# MOM, I WANT YOU TO KNOW

A Guided Journal of Love, Gratitude, and Memories

Written with love for:

*Her laughter lingers in the spaces between our memories, and her love is in every step we take forward.*

Mom, I Want You to Know
Copyright © 2025 Babe Carpenter
All rights reserved.
No part of this book may be copied, reproduced, stored in a retrieval system, or distributed in any form or by any means—electronic, mechanical, photocopying, recording, or otherwise—without the prior written permission of the author, except in the case of brief quotations used in book reviews or educational references.
Published by: Independently Published
This book is intended for personal use and reflection. The author and publisher assume no responsibility for how the content is used or interpreted.

**For my mother,**

There are so many words I wish I could write to you, so many memories I wish I could capture in these pages. But the truth is, no journal could ever hold the depth of love, gratitude, and longing I feel for you.

*Your love shaped me in ways I am still discovering.* Your laughter, your strength, your kindness—they are woven into the fabric of who I am. I carry your lessons with me every day, in the way I love, in the way I give, in the way I hold on to the things that matter.

I only wish I could place this book in your hands, to show you in written words what my heart has always known—you were everything to me. And even now, though you are no longer here, your love is still my guide.

This journal is for all the mothers who give so much and ask for so little. For the moments that deserve to be remembered. For the words that should always be said. And most of all, for you, Mom.

With all my love, always,
Babe

*No matter how time moves forward, a mother's love is the thread that ties our past, present, and future together.*

*There are some words that should never be left unsaid.* Some memories that deserve to be written down, cherished, and passed on. This journal is your space to do just that—to capture the love, gratitude, and moments that make your relationship with your mother so special.

Life moves quickly, and it's easy to assume that the people we love just know how much they mean to us. But time has a way of slipping past, and sometimes, the words left unspoken become the ones we wish we had said the most. This journal is an opportunity to pause, reflect, and express all the things that are in your heart—the memories that make you smile, the lessons that have shaped you, and the appreciation that grows deeper with time.

As you fill these pages, remember that this is not about perfection—it's about honesty, love, and the small details that make your bond with your mother truly unique. There is no right or wrong way to write in this journal. You can fill it in all at once, take your time, or even add to it over the years. What matters most is that these words are written, that they are shared, and that they create something lasting—a keepsake filled with love.

One day, whether it's read now or in the distant future, this journal will serve as a beautiful reminder of the love between you and your mother. A reminder that she is cherished, that her presence has left an incredible mark, and that the connection you share is something truly special.

Take your time, write from your heart, and let this journal be a reflection of the love that will always remain.

With warmth and gratitude,
Babe Carpenter

*A mother's love doesn't need grand gestures—it is in the smallest moments, the quiet sacrifices, and the way she always knows what we need before we do.*

# MOM, I WANT YOU TO KNOW

## How to Use This Journal

This journal is a place to reflect, remember, and express your love for the woman who has shaped your life in countless ways. It is a space to share memories, gratitude, and heartfelt words that will remind her just how much she means to you.

There's no right or wrong way to fill out this book. You can complete it all at once or take your time, letting the memories come naturally. The most important thing is that these words are written—because love, when put into words, becomes a gift that lasts forever.

Here are a few ways to make this journal even more meaningful:

**Write from the heart.** Don't overthink it—this is a space for honesty, love, and appreciation.

**Add personal touches.** Include photos, small mementos, or even a letter to make it extra special.

**Go at your own pace.** You can write a little each day, complete it for a special occasion, or save certain pages for later reflections.

**Give it as a treasured keepsake.** Whether for a birthday, Mother's Day, or just because, this book will hold a love that lasts beyond the pages.

As you fill these pages, remember that every word is a reflection of love—a love that has shaped you, supported you, and will always be a part of who you are.

**Take your time, write your heart, and create something she will cherish forever.**

*The lessons she teaches are not just for today—they are for a lifetime, passed down in whispers, in hugs, in the way love is given freely.*

# MOM, I WANT YOU TO KNOW

Dear Mom,

*There are so many things I want you to know.* Some I may have said before, others I've kept in my heart, waiting for the right moment. This book is my way of sharing those thoughts with you—memories, lessons, and love, all in one place.

From the little moments we shared to the big life lessons you've taught me, you have shaped my world in ways words can barely express. But in these pages, I'm going to try.

This journal is filled with my favorite memories, the things I admire about you, the life lessons I'll always carry with me, and all the love I have for you. I hope that as you read through it, you feel the deep appreciation I have for you—not just today, but always.

So take your time, flip through the pages, smile, laugh, and maybe even shed a happy tear or two. Because this is my way of saying what my heart has always known: You are loved more than words can say.

With all my love,

*A mother's presence is never truly gone. She lives in the stories we tell, the kindness we give, and the love we continue to share.*

Section 1

# Childhood Memories
# &
# Special Moments

# MOM, I WANT YOU TO KNOW

## The earliest memory I have of you is...

#### MOM, I WANT YOU TO KNOW

A time you made me feel really special was when…

# MOM, I WANT YOU TO KNOW

One of my favorite things we used to do together when I was little was…

# MOM, I WANT YOU TO KNOW

## I remember laughing so hard with you when…

# MOM, I WANT YOU TO KNOW

### A tradition you created that I still love today is...

# MOM, I WANT YOU TO KNOW

Something small you did that always made me feel loved was…

# MOM, I WANT YOU TO KNOW

### The best advice you gave me as a child was...

# MOM, I WANT YOU TO KNOW

A time you comforted me when I needed it most was…

# MOM, I WANT YOU TO KNOW

One of my favorite childhood memories with you is...

# MOM, I WANT YOU TO KNOW

A place we used to go together that I'll always remember is...

*No matter how far we go, a mother's love is the home we can always return to.*

Section 2

# Life Lessons
# &
# Your Influence

# MOM, I WANT YOU TO KNOW

One lesson you taught me that I still carry with me is...

# MOM, I WANT YOU TO KNOW

## Something I learned from watching you is…

# MOM, I WANT YOU TO KNOW

The values you instilled in me that I appreciate the most are...

## MOM, I WANT YOU TO KNOW

A moment when I truly understood the depth of your wisdom was...

# MOM, I WANT YOU TO KNOW

The way you handled _____ taught me how to...

# MOM, I WANT YOU TO KNOW

## I admire the way you...

# MOM, I WANT YOU TO KNOW

### The biggest impact you've had on my life is...

# MOM, I WANT YOU TO KNOW

If I could pass one thing you taught me to my future children, it would be…

# MOM, I WANT YOU TO KNOW

A time when I didn't understand your advice, but now I do is...

# MOM, I WANT YOU TO KNOW

You may not realize it, but I learned _____ from you, and it has shaped me in this way...

*No matter how far we go, a mother's love is the home we can always return to.*

# Section 3

# Gratitude & Appreciation

# MOM, I WANT YOU TO KNOW

One thing I don't say enough but want you to know is…

# MOM, I WANT YOU TO KNOW

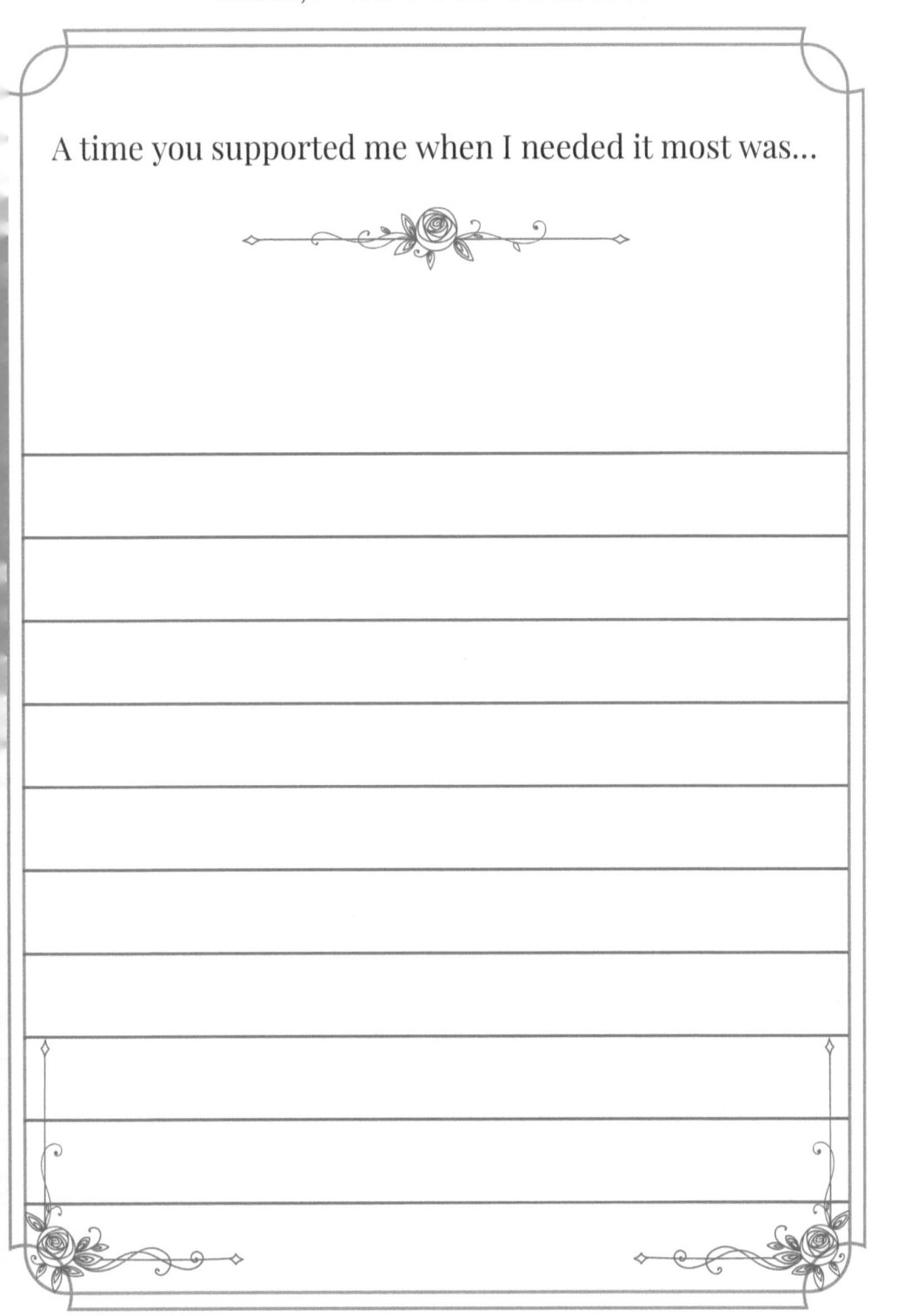

A time you supported me when I needed it most was…

# MOM, I WANT YOU TO KNOW

## I'm grateful for you because...

# MOM, I WANT YOU TO KNOW

You have a special way of making people feel…

# MOM, I WANT YOU TO KNOW

Something you do that I will always cherish is...

# MOM, I WANT YOU TO KNOW

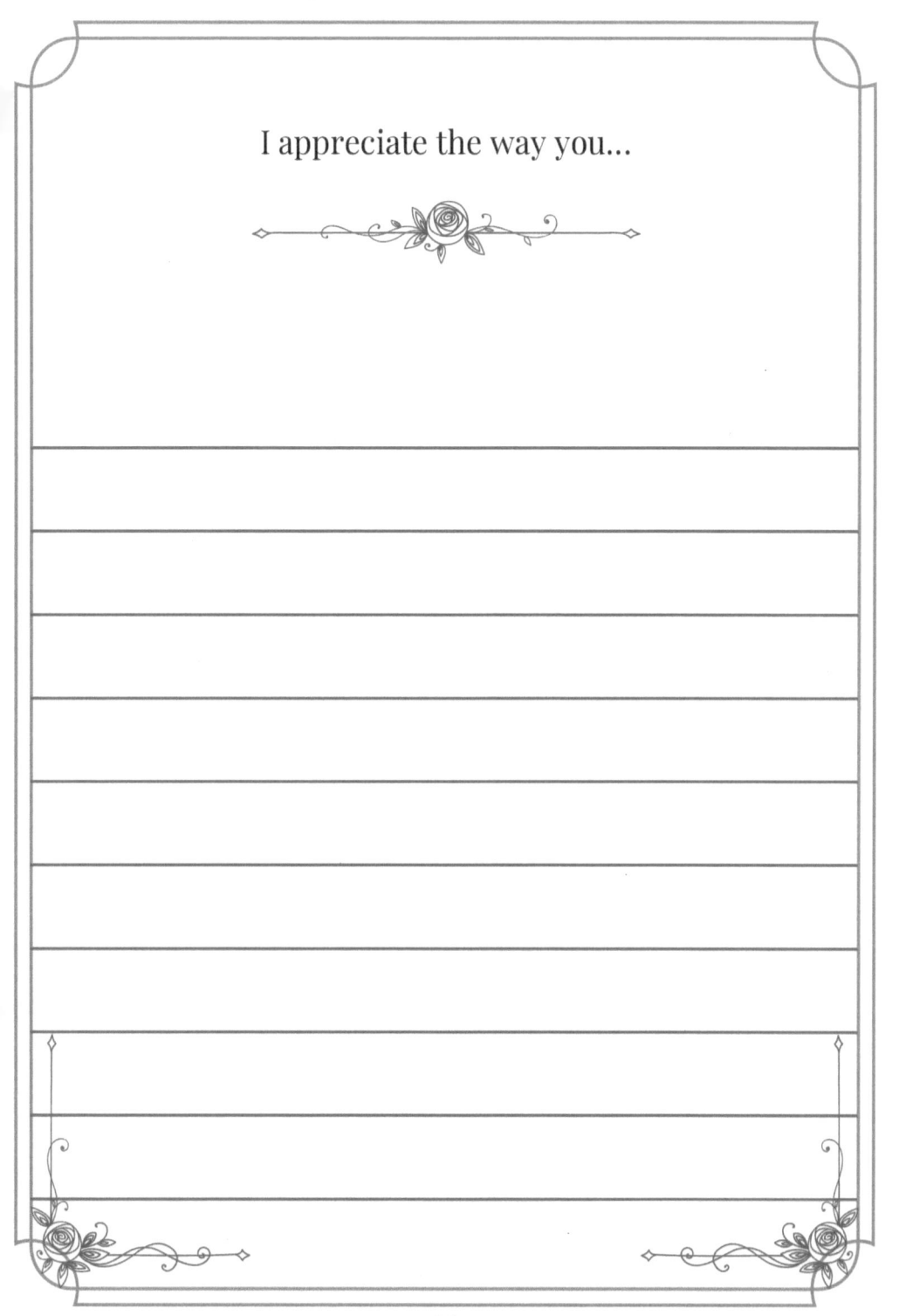

## I appreciate the way you...

# MOM, I WANT YOU TO KNOW

You might not even remember this, but a small act of kindness you did that meant so much to me was...

# MOM, I WANT YOU TO KNOW

If I could give you one gift to show you what you mean to me, it would be…

## MOM, I WANT YOU TO KNOW

A moment when I realized just how amazing you are was...

One thing you've done that changed my life is…

# MOM, I WANT YOU TO KNOW

A time when you believed in me, even when I doubted myself, was…

Section 4

# A Love Letter to You

*"If love could be written in words, it would fill endless pages—but even then, it could never capture all that you mean to me. This letter is just a glimpse of the love that has always been here, the gratitude that grows with time, and the bond that no distance, no years, and no words left unsaid could ever break."*

# MOM, I WANT YOU TO KNOW

"Dear Mom, if I haven't said it enough, I want you to know..."

# MOM, I WANT YOU TO KNOW

Section 5

# Keepsakes
# &
# Special Additions

*Her love is not just in the past—it is in every decision we make, every kindness we offer, and every dream she believed in before we could see it ourselves.*

MOM, I WANT YOU TO KNOW

My favorite photos of us...

*A mother's love is the quiet kind of magic—the kind that turns ordinary days into cherished moments, and simple words into a lifelong embrace.*

# MOM, I WANT YOU TO KNOW

My favorite photos of us...

*She is the keeper of our childhood, the holder of our dreams, and the one whose love never fades, only grows deeper with time.*

My favorite photos of us...

# MOM, I WANT YOU TO KNOW

A special song that reminds me of you…

# MOM, I WANT YOU TO KNOW

## Something I hope we always do together is...

# MOM, I WANT YOU TO KNOW

## A wish I have for your future is...

# MOM, I WANT YOU TO KNOW

If I could bottle up one moment with you and keep it forever, it would be...

*Some lessons are spoken, some are shown, but a mother's love is felt in every moment, whether near or far.*

Section 6

# Things I Love Most About You

# MOM, I WANT YOU TO KNOW

## Top 5 Things I Love Most About You

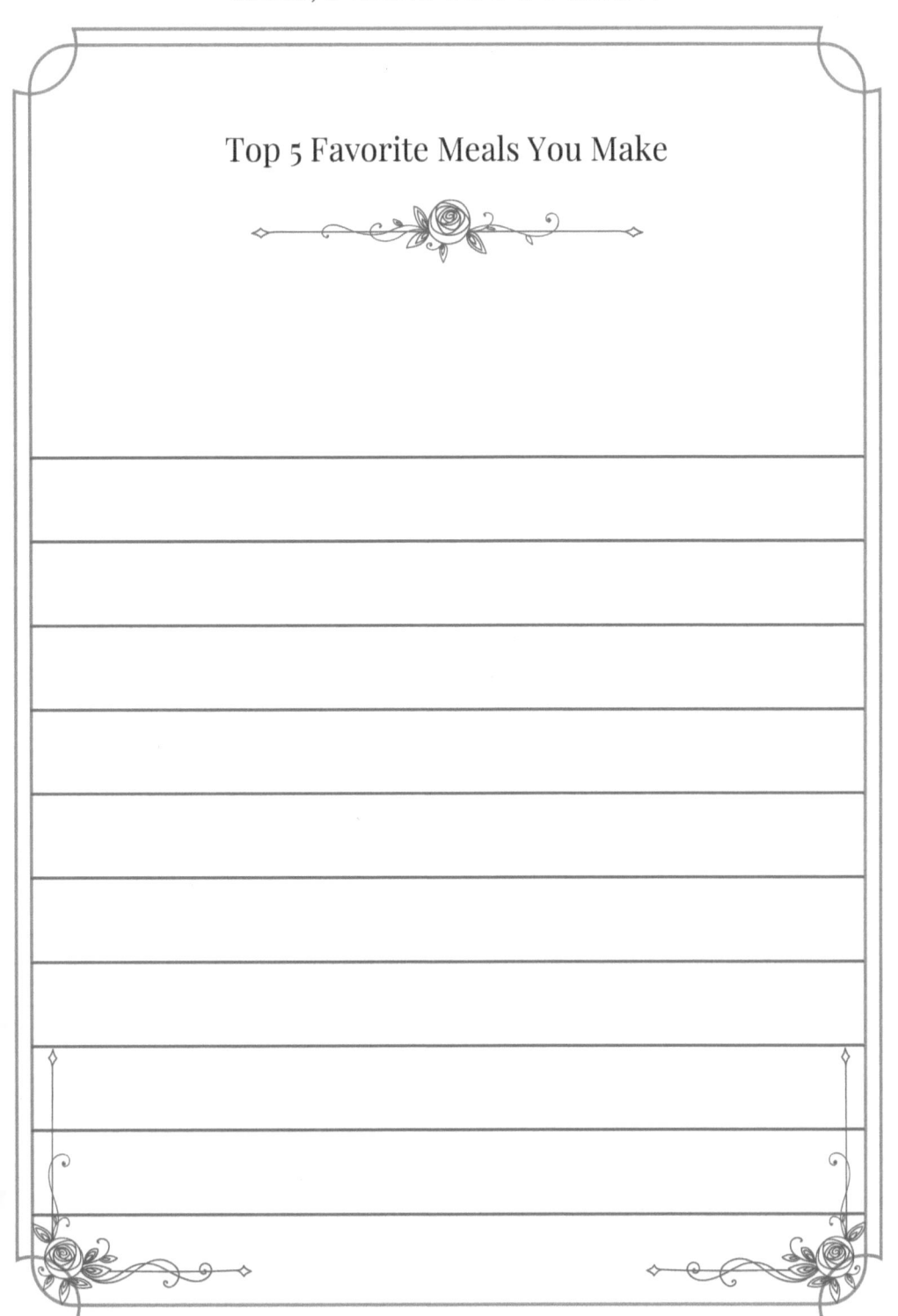

# MOM, I WANT YOU TO KNOW

## Top 5 Favorite Meals You Make

# MOM, I WANT YOU TO KNOW

## Top 5 Things You've Taught Me

# MOM, I WANT YOU TO KNOW

## Top 5 Funniest Moments We've Shared

# MOM, I WANT YOU TO KNOW

## If I Had to Describe You in One Word, It Would Be...

" _____

_____ "

# MOM, I WANT YOU TO KNOW

## You Always Know How to Make Me Feel...

# MOM, I WANT YOU TO KNOW

## I Will Never Forget When You...

# MOM, I WANT YOU TO KNOW

## A Little Thing You Do That Means So Much to Me Is...

# MOM, I WANT YOU TO KNOW

## I Want You to Know That I Will Always...

72

# MOM, I WANT YOU TO KNOW

## One Day, I Hope We Can...

# MOM, I WANT YOU TO KNOW

## You Might Not Realize It, But I Learned _____ From You, and It Has Helped Me...

MOM, I WANT YOU TO KNOW

## The Best Hug You Ever Gave Me Was When...

## MOM, I WANT YOU TO KNOW

### The Funniest Advice You Ever Gave Me Was…

Section 7

# MOM
# Guess My Answers

## Mom, Guess My Answers...

---

What do you think is one thing I admire most about you?

    Mom's Guess: _____

    My Answer: _____

What's something funny we both always laugh about?

    Mom's Guess: _____

    My Answer: _____

If I could take you on a dream vacation, where do you think I'd choose?

    Mom's Guess: _____

    My Answer: _____

What do you think is my favorite childhood memory with you?

    Mom's Guess: _____

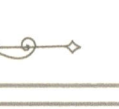

    My Answer: _____

Section 8

# MOM
# You Inspire Me Because

# MOM, I WANT YOU TO KNOW

## Mom, you inspire me because...

# MOM, I WANT YOU TO KNOW

## The strength I admire most in you is...

# MOM, I WANT YOU TO KNOW

When I think of your creativity/patience/kindness, I feel…

# MOM, I WANT YOU TO KNOW

One of the greatest lessons you taught me, without even realizing it, was…

*A mother's love is written in the little things—warm meals, gentle hands, and a heart that always says, "I'm here."*

Section 9

# Our Bucket List: Adventures For Us

# MOM, I WANT YOU TO KNOW

One adventure I dream of sharing with you is...

# MOM, I WANT YOU TO KNOW

## A special tradition I'd love for us to start is...

# MOM, I WANT YOU TO KNOW

One goal I have for us in the coming years is...

# MOM, I WANT YOU TO KNOW

One adventure I would love for us to experience together is...

# MOM, I WANT YOU TO KNOW

## Mom's Bucket List...

Section 10

# Final Thoughts

# MOM, I WANT YOU TO KNOW

## Filling out this journal made me realize...

# MOM, I WANT YOU TO KNOW

What I hope you feel when reading this is...

# MOM, I WANT YOU TO KNOW

## The greatest gift you've given me is...

# MOM, I WANT YOU TO KNOW

**To the one filling out this journal,**

As you turned these pages, I hope you felt the depth of love, gratitude, and memories that have shaped your life. Writing these words is more than just filling in blanks—it is a way of capturing moments that might otherwise slip away, a way of saying things that should never be left unsaid. One day, these words will be a gift, a reminder of the love that existed between you and your mother, a love that is felt in every shared smile, every quiet sacrifice, and every lesson passed down.

**To Mom,**

If I could, I would have written these words for my own mother. But time does not wait, and life does not always give us the chance to say everything our hearts hold. If you are reading this, know that you are loved in ways too deep for words, and that your presence has shaped a life in ways you may never fully see. This journal is just a small reflection of that love—a keepsake of all the moments, big and small, that make you irreplaceable.

May these pages bring you joy, laughter, and the reassurance that your love is not only felt today but will live on for generations to come.

With all my heart,

Made in United States
Troutdale, OR
05/04/2025